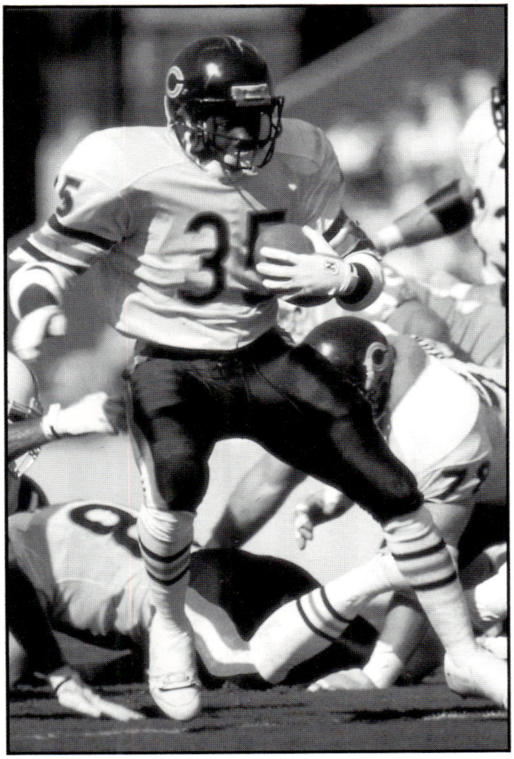

CHICAGO BEARS

Pat Ryan

CREATIVE EDUCATION INC.

Published by Creative Education, Inc.
123 S. Broad Street, Mankato, Minnesota 56001

Designed by Rita Marshall
Cover illustration by Lance Hidy Associates
Photos by Allsport, Bettmann Archives, Duomo, Focus
On Sports, Spectra-Action and Wide World Photos

Copyright © 1991 Creative Education, Inc.
International copyrights reserved in all countries.
No part of this book may be reproduced in any form
without written permission from the publisher.
Printed in the United States of America

Library of Congress Cataloging-in-Publication Data

Ryan, Pat.
  Chicago Bears/Pat Ryan.
  p. cm.
  ISBN 0-88682-361-7
  1. Chicago Bears (Football team)—History. I. Title.
GV956.C5R93   1990
796.332'64'0977311—dc20   90-41541
                                        CIP

"Papa Bear" George Halas (far right).

October 16, 1921, was like many other Sundays in Chicago. It was a beautiful autumn afternoon in the city. Most families were enjoying a break from what was then a six-day workweek. Many were spending their time in the parks or strolling along Lake Michigan. But for one young man this would not be a day of rest but a day in which he would introduce his professional football team, the Chicago Bears, to the people of the Windy City.

George Halas was up early preparing for the game. The contest was to be played at Cubs Park, and the cost of a ticket was one dollar. Only twenty-six years old, Halas was hoping that enough people would show up that day so he could meet expenses.

Arriving by streetcar, by Model T, and by foot, nearly 8,000 spectators would come to support the team in midnight blue and orange. Halas was pleasantly surprised by the outpouring of fan support.

1921

Legendary coach George Halas guided the Bears to a 10-1-1 record.

PAPA BEAR

Many people believe Chicago sports fans are the greatest in the world. No one felt this more strongly than the man they called "Papa Bear," George Halas. In 1921, after the Staley Starch Company dropped its sponsorship of the semi-pro team, the Decatur Staleys, Halas and his partner, Dutch Sternaman, took a chance on this belief. They bought the team, moved it to Chicago, and renamed the club the Chicago Bears.

Five years later, Halas gained complete control of the club and it has been an overwhelming success ever since. As the leader of the Bears, Halas became a man of action. He could sell tickets, tape ankles, shovel snow, coach, and occasionally play defense. In one game, he put himself in the contest at defensive end. Minutes later he scooped up a fumble by the legendary Jim Thorpe and raced a record ninety-eight yards for a Chicago touchdown.

Halas was a man of many firsts. He was the first National Football League coach to schedule daily practices, the first to study game films, and the first to introduce a team song. It was also Halas's idea to change the name of the football league from the American Professional Football

Walter Payton, the NFL's all-time leading rusher.

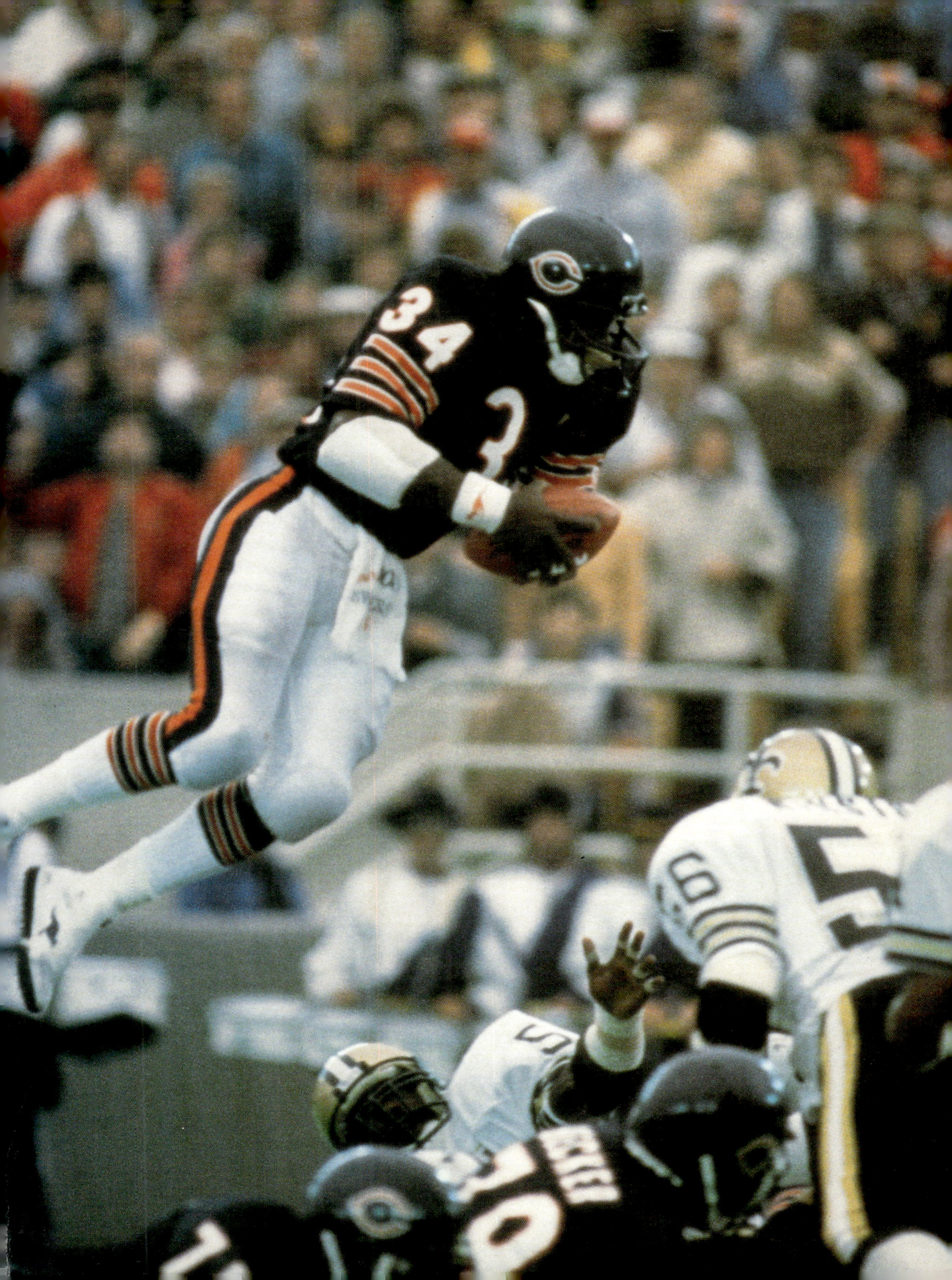

Big Bucks! Red Grange signed a contract with the Bears for the astronomical sum of $100,000!

1925

Association to the NFL. But above all, Halas was the first man to dream that football could become a first-class, big-league sport.

It would only take a few short years and two giant running backs to help make Halas's dream become a reality. The addition of Red Grange and Bronco Nagurski, between 1925 and 1930, changed the fortunes of the Chicago Bears and the face of professional football forever.

Red Grange, known as the "Galloping Ghost," signed with Halas and the Bears on November 22, 1925. Immediately after joining the team, Halas arranged a cross-country tour to show off his new superstar. From New York to Los Angeles they traveled. Nineteen cities in less than six months. For Red Grange it was a hectic beginning to a very successful career.

In all, Grange would play professional football for thirteen seasons. Yet, because no accurate records were kept in the early 1920s, the Galloping Ghost is not listed among the top twenty-five ground-gainers in Bear history. But even if statistics had been gathered Grange's achievements could not be measured in numbers. "I wouldn't say he was the greatest back I've ever known," wrote Grantland Rice. "Not with Bronco Nagurski and Jim Thorpe around. But in my opinion, Red had more influence on the pro game than any other player. He made the game the success that it is."

Helping the Bears and Grange reach new levels of success by the 1930s was Bronislau Nagurski. Nagurski, who joined the team for the 1930 season, was an immediate sensation. He was a league all-star in his very first year. Better known as Bronco, this irresistible force played seven seasons for Chicago between 1930 and 1943. During this period his bone-jarring runs and hardnosed style became a thing of legend.

In one game, Nagurski blasted through two tacklers, through the end zone, and full speed into the brick retaining wall behind it. Shaking his head, which was covered by a flimsy leather helmet, Nagurski trotted back to the bench and remarked, "That last guy really gave me a good lick."

Not many things could stop Nagurski, Grange and the Bears in the early 1930s. Between 1932 and 1934 Chicago dominated the NFL, winning two consecutive championships (1932 and 1933). Through the remainder of the 1930s, however, the brilliance faded. The young stars—Nagurski and Grange—became battered veterans and slowly saw their careers come to an end. Though Father Time finally caught up with them, the Galloping Ghost and Bronco were destined for the Hall of Fame.

Running back Bronco Nagurski pounded out 529 yards rushing during the season.

A QUARTERBACK LEADS THE WAY

With Chicago's legends in the twilight of their careers, Halas was pressed to find someone to lead the Bears back to the top. Papa Bear wanted someone who could produce perfection. The owner of the Bears would work wonders by converting Sid Luckman, a runner, into a quarterback.

Luckman, who played his college ball as a tailback at Columbia, became a master of the T-formation. From 1940 to 1943, Luckman led the Bears to an incredible 37-5-1 record.

Like Sid Luckman, Jim McMahon quarterbacked the Bears to a world championship. (pages 10—11)

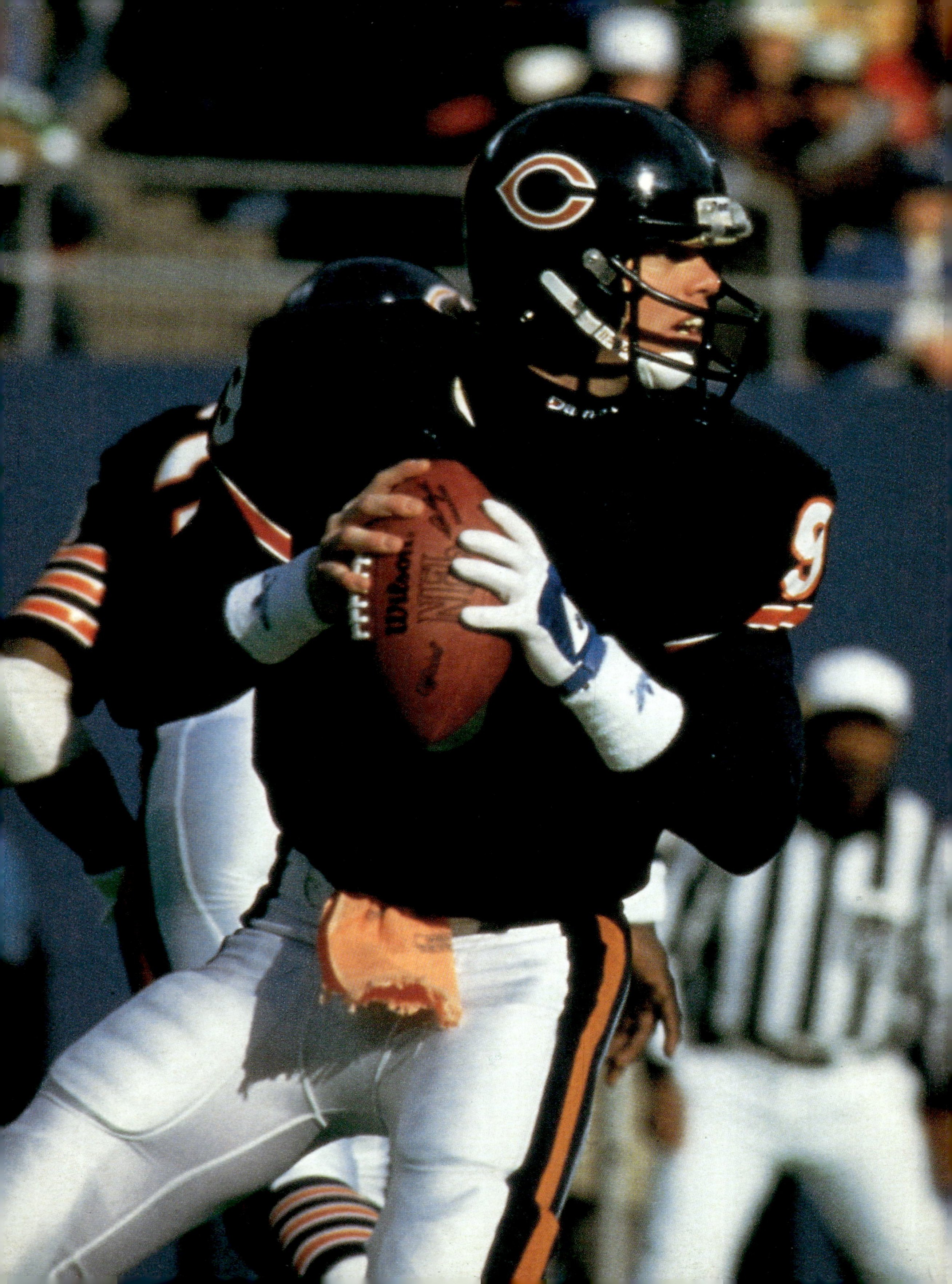

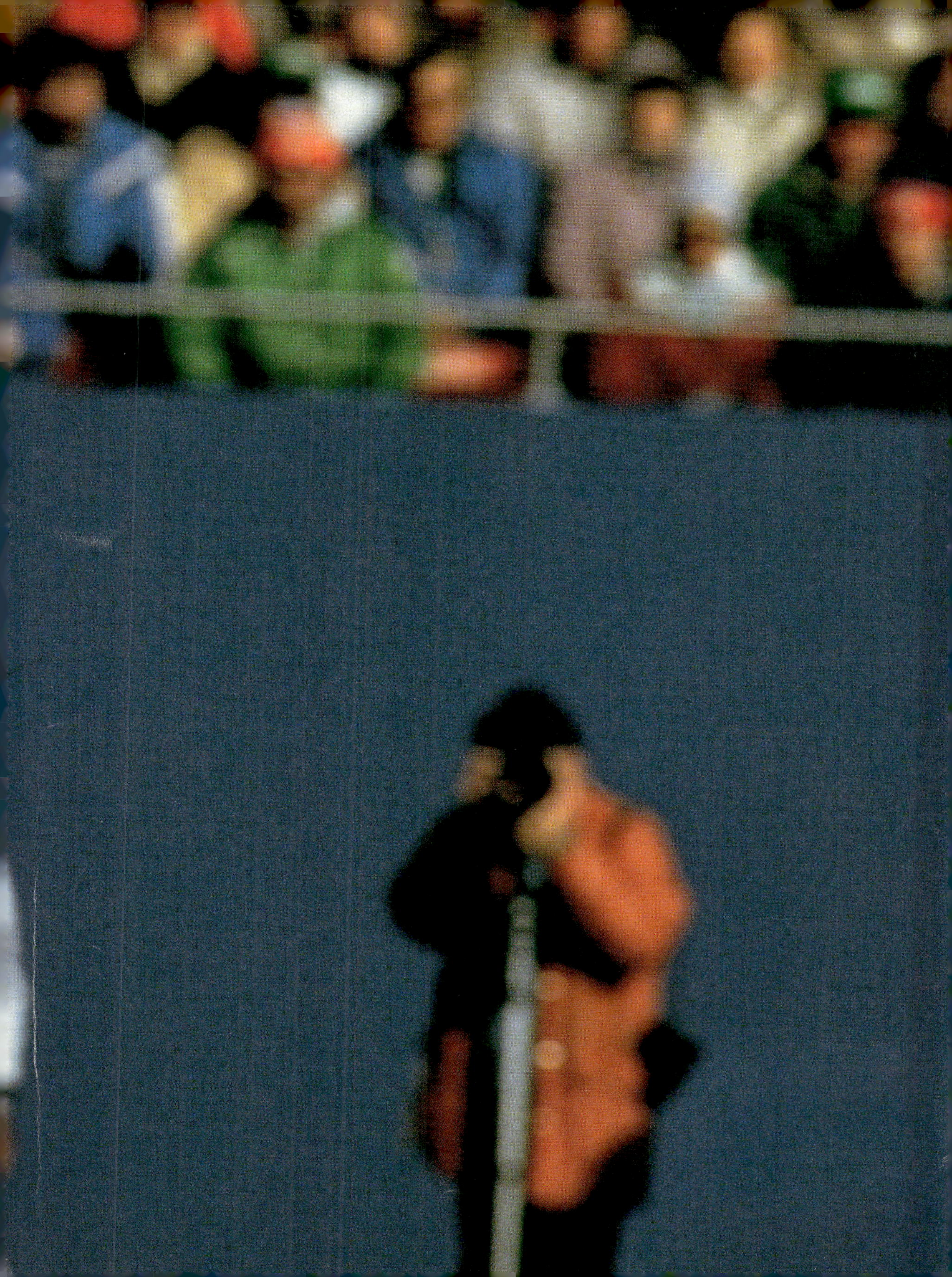

1 9 4 0

The Bears' championship team would have been even better with the incomparable Gale Sayers (right).

Perfection in any endeavor is difficult, but the idea of a perfect football team seemed impossible. But the Chicago squad of 1940 seemed close. The Bears were voted the greatest professional team of all time by the National Academy of Sports Editors in 1963. It was the championship game that convinced many of the writers. And it was Halas again who provided the motivation.

The Bears had played the Washington Redskins earlier in the year and lost 7-3 on a controversial call. When the Bears complained, the Redskins' owner, George Marshall, told the press that "the Bears were quitters and a bunch of cry babies."

Halas was furious. He took the press clippings and plastered the locker room walls with the quotation. Halas then gave an inspiring pep talk. He ended it by saying, "Gentlemen, this is what the Redskins think of you, I think you're a great football team, the greatest ever assembled. Go out onto the field and prove it."

The fired-up Bears destroyed the Redskins 73-0 before 36,000 quiet Redskin fans. It got so bad that at one point an official approached Halas and asked if he would try not to kick any more extra points. So many balls had been booted into the stands and taken by fans as souvenirs that the Redskins were down to their last football!

The Bears' lineup for that championship game included three future Hall of Famers—Luckman, George McAfee, and Joe Stydahar. The record seventy-three points still stands today as the most points scored in any NFL regular-season, play-off, or championship game.

"Some observers said the Bears were a perfect football team that day," recalled Halas. "I can't quite agree. Looking over the movies, I can see where we should have scored another touchdown."

From 1947 to 1951, the Bears produced more winning seasons, but injuries robbed them of championships. Luckman would retire in 1951; fourteen years later he was inducted into the Hall of Fame.

The Chicago football fans would never totally abandon their team, but from 1952 to 1962 the Bears fell from favor. Not all of the teams were terrible, but even the winning teams couldn't provide consistency, and for fans who were used to winning, the times were hard.

Players like Rick Casares, Willie Galimore, and Bobby Watkins were great, but they couldn't seem to make a difference. One name could make a difference, and that name was Halas. Papa Bear had given up his title as coach

Sid Luckman became the first professional quarterback to pass for over 400 yards in a game.

Linebacker Dick Butkus grabbed five interceptions and recovered six fumbles in his rookie season.

so he could manage the front office but now it was time to return to the sidelines. Papa Bear would be calling the plays once again.

In just a few short years, the Bears were clawing their way back into contention. In 1963, with a new defensive coordinator by the name of George Allen, the Bears were back in the thick of the title race. And by season's end the Bears had finished one-half game ahead of Vince Lombardi's Packers.

In the title game, Halas's boys were the underdogs. Their opponent, the New York Giants, were led by Y. A. Tittle and Frank Gifford. But Chicago put forth a heroic effort and defeated the Giants by intercepting five of Tittle's passes on their way to a 14-10 victory. The NFL championship trophy was back in Chicago after a seventeen-year absence.

TWO OF THE BEST

While Halas was reestablishing his dynasty, Lombardi, in Green Bay, was building his own. Undaunted, Halas went back to his strength, drafting superstars. The 1965 draft would prove to be one of the best ever for the Bears. Like Grange and Nagurski, his picks would be a combination of finesse and brute force.

George Halas signed linebacker Dick Butkus from Illinois and running back Gale Sayers from Kansas. The swift Sayers would provide the finesse and the fearsome Butkus would provide the brute force.

Dick Butkus was notorious for his hard hitting. He loved to hit so much that sometimes he forgot that the goal was to win. In one contest, with the Bears down by three

Linebacker Dick Butkus.

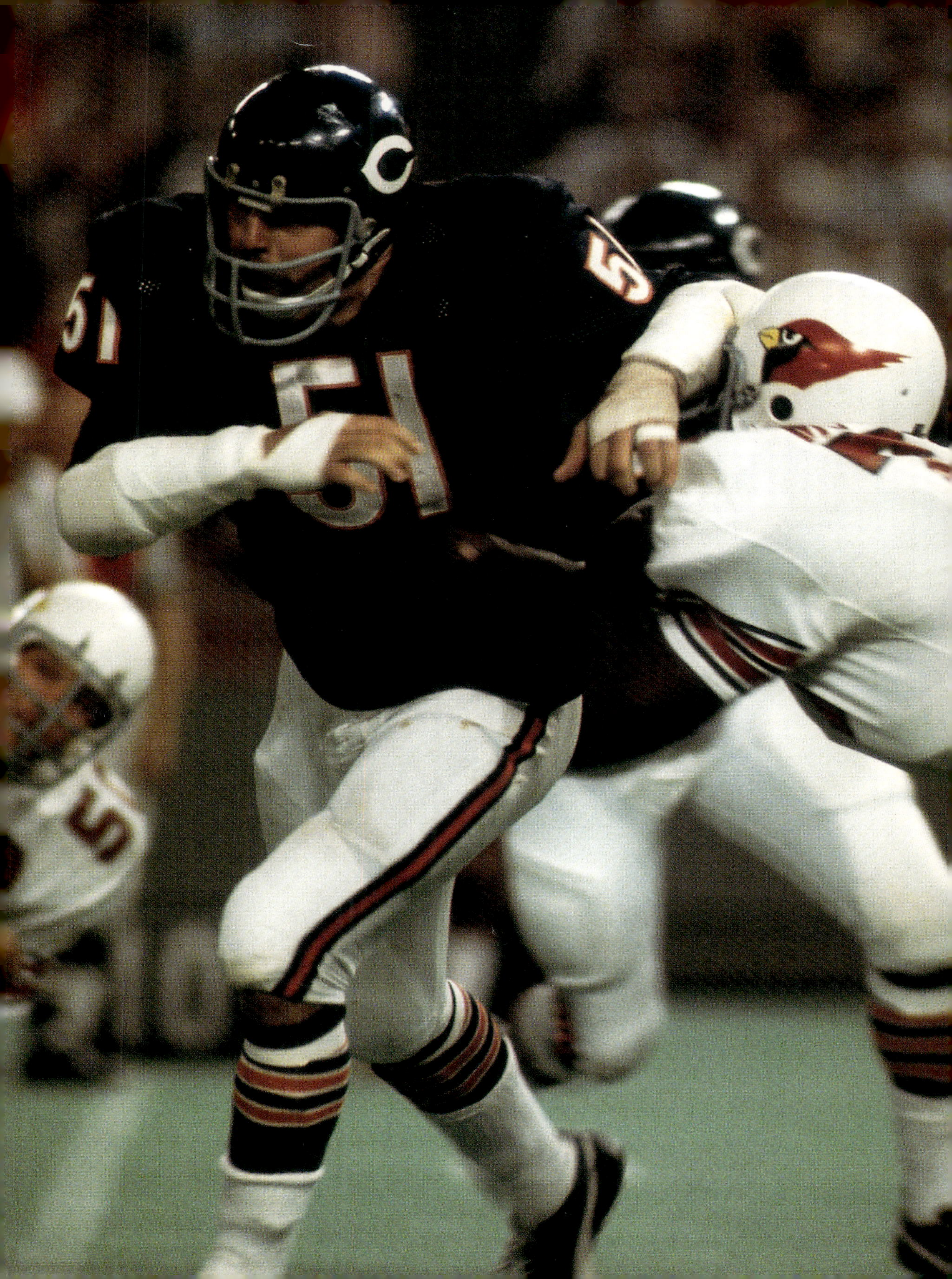

Gale Sayers led the NFL by rushing for over 1200 yards during the season.

touchdowns, Butkus called a time-out with just a few seconds remaining in the game. Most of the players expected the clock to run out; after all, it was a blowout. They wanted to go to the showers. Later, when asked about the time-out, Butkus replied, "I just wanted one more chance to hit somebody."

"Butkus was the epitome of the middle linebacker" said Mike Ditka. "He played the game from the tip of his head to the bottom of his soles." Although the Bears were struggling, the individual play of Butkus gave the fans something to cheer about.

In 1971 number 51 was inducted into the Hall of Fame in his first year of eligibility. In his career Butkus was All-NFL eight times and played in eight Pro Bowls.

Gale Sayers, too, would be elected to the Hall in his first year of eligibility. Sayers was a running back in the Bear tradition of Grange and Nagurski. In Sayer's rookie season, he became a nightmare for defensive backs. "He's no different than any other runner when he's coming at you," quipped a San Francisco 49er defensive back, "but when he gets there he's gone."

"He detects daylight," explained Halas. "The average back, when he sees a hole, will try to bull his way through. But Gale if the hole is even partly clogged, instinctively takes off in the opposite direction. And he does it so swiftly and surely that the defense is usually left frozen. He has wonderful speed. And he can lull you into thinking he is going all out, then turns it up another notch and he's gone."

In a seven year career, cut short by a knee injury, Sayers continued to amaze each and every season. His ability to start and stop on a dime left defenders grasping. In all,

In the 1980s Mike Singletary's fierce play reminded many of Dick Butkus.

Tough defense is a Chicago Bear trademark.

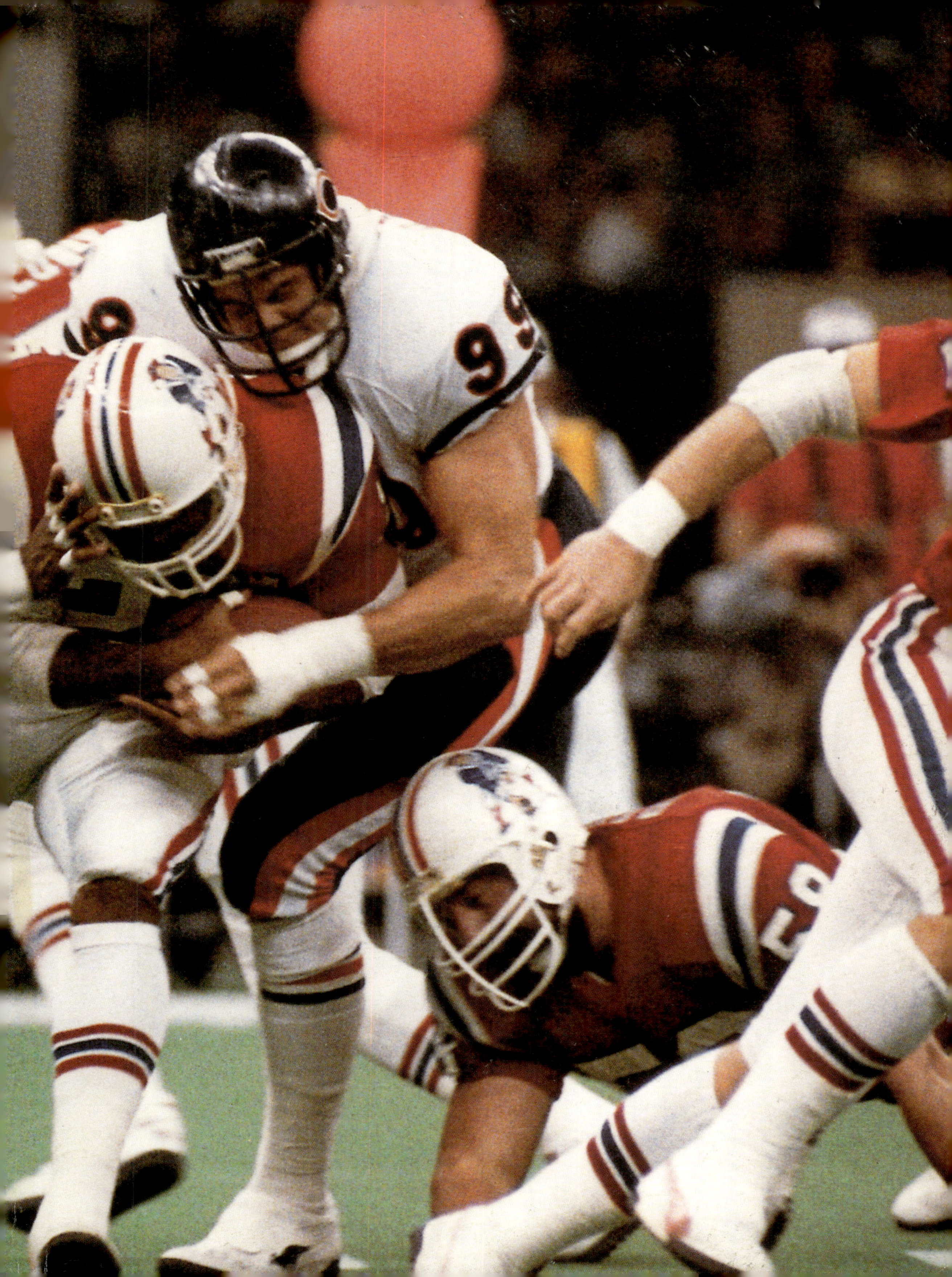

Gale gained nearly 5000 yards rushing in a Chicago uniform. He was truly one the most electrifying players to ever carry a football.

SWEETNESS

The late sixties and early seventies became a period of great players rather than years of play-off games. Bear fans enjoyed the big plays of Butkus, Sayers, Doug Plant, and Vince Evans, but the records were not good. Coach Abe Gibron was 11-30-1 in his three years and Jack Pardee was 20-22 from 1975 to 1978. Following this trend the decade would close with the acquisition of one of the greatest backs of all time—the man they called "Sweetness," Walter Jerry Payton.

"Wonderful Walter" was born and raised in Columbia, Mississippi. Walter spent most of his childhood living in the shadow of his older brother, Eddie. Eddie was supposed to be the athlete in the family. In high school, Walter didn't go out for football until after Eddie had graduated. In the meantime, Walter satisfied his competitive need to perform by playing drums in the school band and by joining the gymnastics team.

"Walter was the real serious type of a child," Mrs. Payton recalled. "He'd rather stay in the house with me and read or help me with the chores when his brother was playing football. But when Walter began playing the game, he was stubborn, and good." In Walter's first high school game he ran for a sixty-one-yard touchdown.

After a four-year college career at Jackson State, Payton continued his excellence as a professional. As a member

1977

Walter Payton led the Bears to their first play-off appearance in fourteen years.

of the Chicago Bears he was a player who performed feats of magical entertainment. One of the most memorable acts of magic came on a cold, damp day in Chicago, in November of 1977.

The 50,000 fans who came to Soldier Field that day were shivering and wet, but they were rewarded with one of the most exciting games ever played by their favorite running back. This was the day Payton galloped for 275 yards, the most rushing yardage gained by any man in a single game in the history of professional football.

The twenty-three-year old Payton had become a star in only his rookie season. But it was only the beginning of many great things to come. Over the next eleven years Sweetness would become the most prolific rusher in NFL history. His powerful and determined running would make him one of the greatest players to ever play football.

The shy and quiet Payton remained humble throughout his record-setting career. He always gave credit to his linemen and at one point gave each of them an engraved gold watch. Walter was happy about his successes, but as a pro football player he knew that there was one prize and one prize only, the "ring." The Super Bowl ring. This was one honor, however, that Walter could not win alone.

Bears' quarterback Vince Evans passed for over 2300 yards during the season.

THE DITKA YEARS

The roller-coaster years of the seventies eventually gave way to a new era. Once again it was led by the vision of George Halas. Chicago needed to find a man who had the drive to take the Bears to the top. Ever since Halas's retirement from coaching in 1968, the team had not been

Matt Suhey (#26) was a key player in the 1980s.

able to turn the corner to consistent play. They needed someone who was a Bear—a man who could take the team into the eighties.

Not everyone was high on Halas's choice. Many people thought Mike Ditka was too emotional to lead any team. Papa Bear did not agree. Halas knew that Ditka, an ex-Bear himself, could fire up his team. He knew Ditka could instill the spirit of the old championship teams. "I was always a Bear," admitted Ditka. "Even when I was playing and coaching in Dallas, I was a Chicago Bear." Iron Mike was home, and a winning team was just around the corner.

Ditka had a wealth of talent waiting for him when he arrived. Quality players like defensive end Dan Hampton, safety Gary Fencik, linebacker Mike Singletary, and of course, Walter. Ditka's job was to take these thoroughbreds to the race and win.

But before Ditka could make his mark tragedy struck. On October 31, 1983, George Halas, the winningest professional coach of all time, died of a massive heart attack. The one they called Papa Bear was gone, and the organization would never be the same. George Halas knew how to win. In his career as a coach, he had won an incredible 326 games.

Halas's death jolted the Bears back into championship form. In both 1983 and 1984 Chicago captured the Central Division title. Although they fell short of their ultimate goal, the Super Bowl, the Bears were poised for greatness.

One Bear who had already achieved greatness, Walter Payton, accomplished several other milestones in 1984. Sweetness surpassed Jim Brown as the NFL's all time

Coach Mike Ditka guided the Bears to their first of five consecutive Central division titles.

24 *Clockwise: Neal Anderson, William Perry, Vestee Jackson, Mike Singletary.*

leading rusher. In addition, he became the career leader in 100-yard games and set a Chicago team reception mark.

What fun the entire Chicago team had in 1985. The Bears won their first twelve games of the year en route to a 15-1 record. The fifteen wins tied an NFL mark for most wins during the regular season.

But the Bears didn't stop there. In the first round of the play-offs they shut down Joe Gibbs and the Washington Redskins 21-0. Their next opponent, for the NFC championship, was the Los Angeles Rams. Once again the fearsome Bear defense shut the door and quarterback Jim McMahon and the offense followed through giving the Bears a 24-0 win. The next stop was New Orleans and the Super Bowl.

In Super Bowl XX, the Bears faced the New England Patriots. It had been quite a year for the Bears. Now many people were wondering if Ditka could pull off the big game. They weren't wondering for long. The Bears quickly choked the life out of the Patriots. They set seven Super Bowl records in the process, including most points, forty-six and the largest margin of victory, thirty-six. Walter Payton finally had his ring.

From 1986 through 1988 the Chicago Bears continued to dominate play in the NFC Central Division. Under Ditka's leadership they won three more division championships. Of course talented players like Singletary, McMahon, Hampton, Payton and Richard Dent made Ditka's job much easier.

In the five year period between 1984 and 1988 this cast of players won sixty-two games. The most ever by an NFL

1 9 8 6

Super Bowl, Super Play: Quarterback Jim McMahon passed for 250 yards and rushed for two touchdowns.

William Perry (#72) and teammates, (pages 26–27).

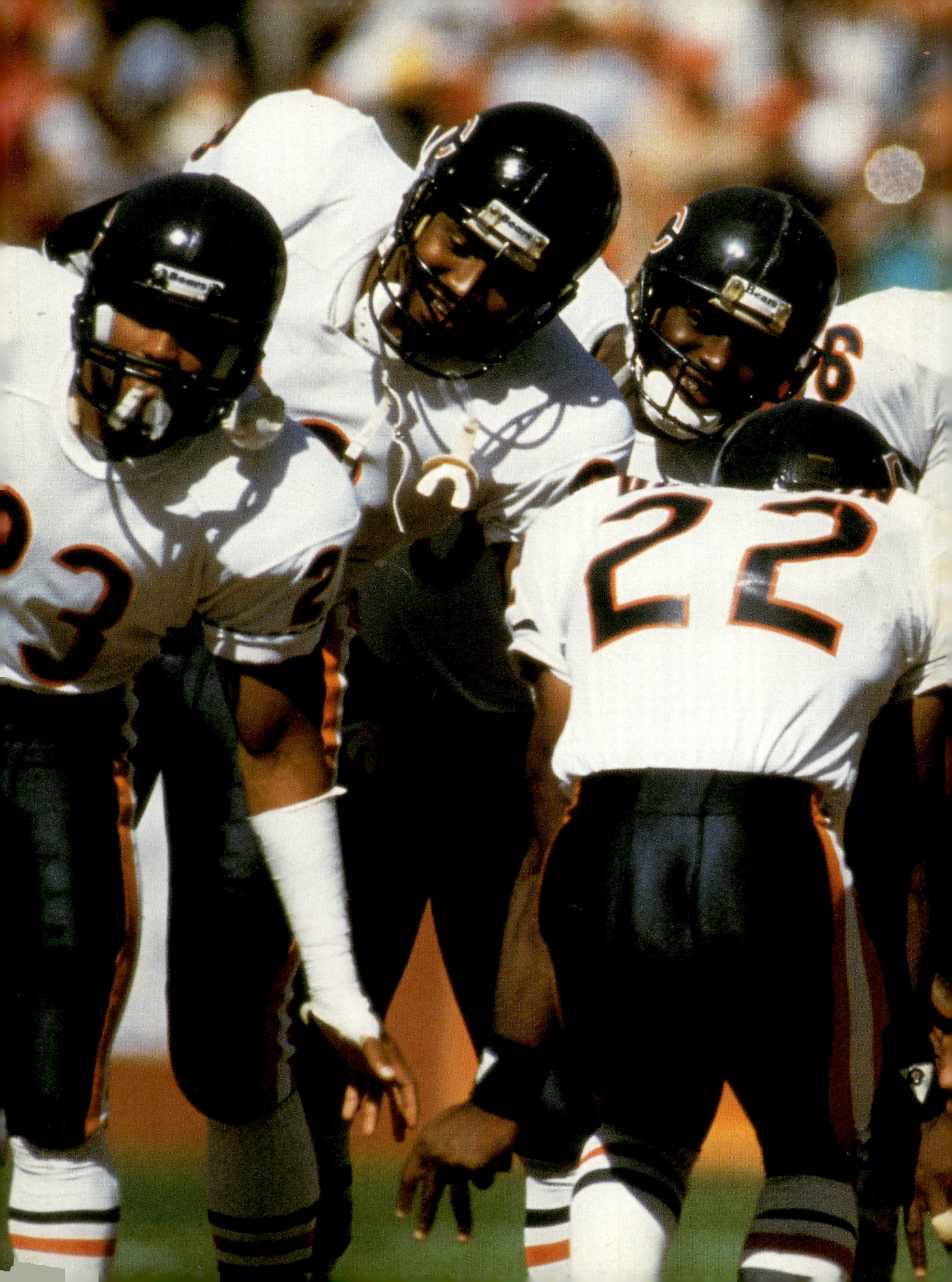
22

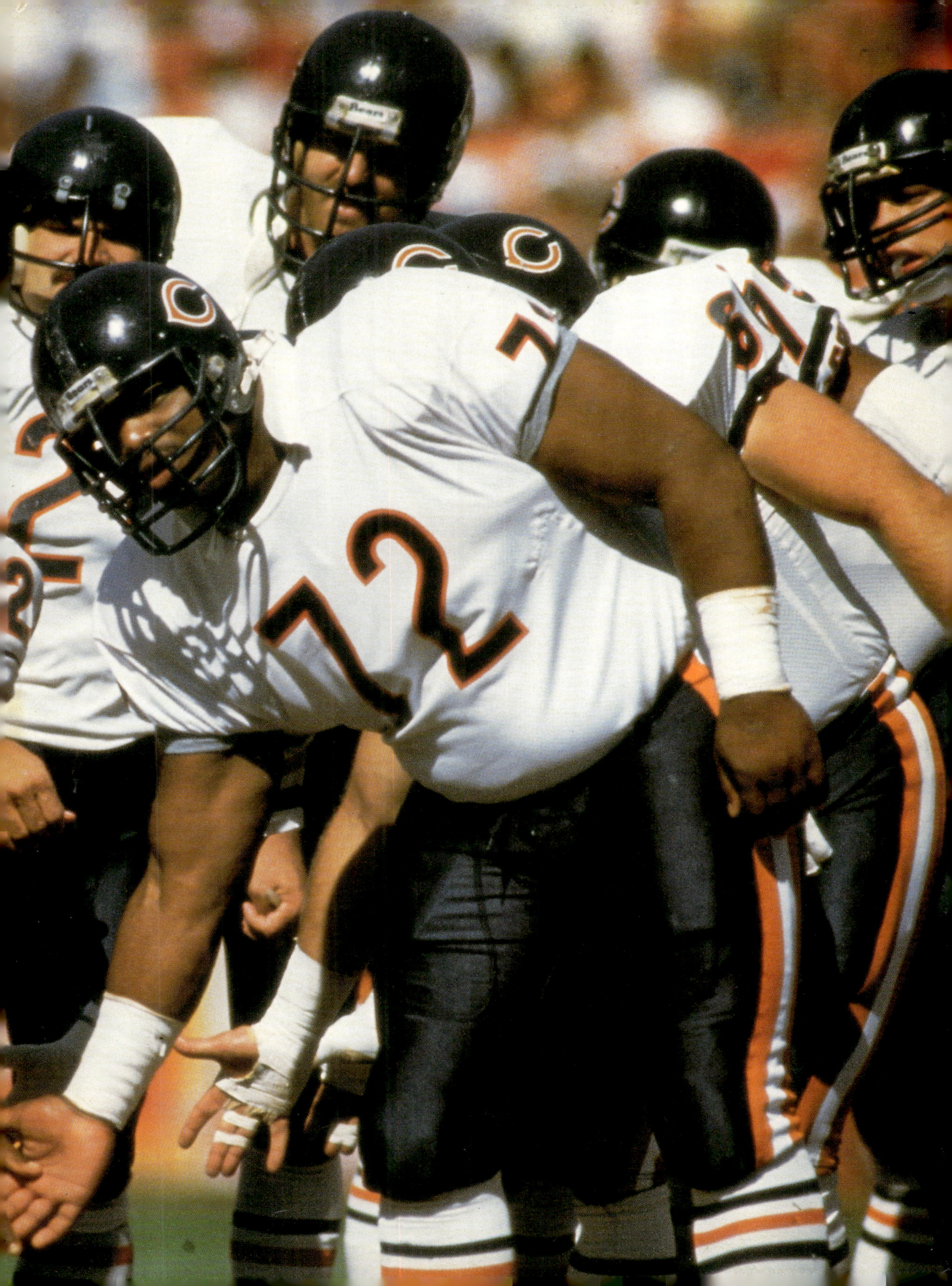
72

squad. Yet despite all this success, the Bears were unable to achieve what they most wanted—another Super Bowl championship.

HEADING INTO THE NINETIES

Even though the Bears underwent several changes as the decade of the eighties came to a close, including the retirement of Payton and the trading of McMahon, Chicago remained a strong team. In the all-important kicking game, Ditka had Kevin Butler, one of the best in the game, who in 1989 set a record for the most consecutive field goals. Butler is the Bears' all-time leader in field goal accuracy, 73.8 percent. Butler is young and will no doubt be kicking balls well into the nineties.

Ditka has another talented Bear in the backfield in Neal Anderson. In 1990 the Bears signed Neal Anderson to a multiyear contract. Anderson, who played his college ball at Florida, was drafted in 1986 and has been the workhorse for the Bears since Walter Payton's retirement. He first impressed the Bears coaching staff with his efforts on the special teams, but in 1987 he became the starting fullback. Since then Anderson has carried the ball over 40 percent of the time. Today, he remains the most durable back in the offense.

But he is not alone. Anderson is joined in the backfield by Brad Muster out of Stanford and reserve Thomas Sanders. The Bears have traditionally been a great rushing team, and that part of their game is in place for the future.

The Bears' quarterback position has always been filled by fiercely competitive men who aren't happy sitting on the bench. McMahon was traded to San Diego in 1989, and

Mr. Pro Bowl! Defensive captain Mike Singletary was named to his eighth consecutive Pro Bowl.

Running back Neal Anderson.

Placekicker Kevin Butler.

The Bears' leader of the '90s, Jim Harbaugh (#14).

Mike Tomczak and Jim Harbaugh stepped in to take over the leadership duties for the nineties. Ditka believes either player can win and win soon. Ditka doesn't like the excuse "it's a transition year," so look for the Bears to be back in championship form in the nineties.

The Chicago Bears, like their founder George Halas, have always been fighters. Win or lose the Monsters of the Midway always put up a battle. It has been that way since Grange and Nagurski; and will continue into the nineties with Anderson, Singletary and the rest of the big, bad Bears.

CLEVELAND MIDDLE SCHOOL
Instructional Media Center
1000 Walsh St. Paul, MN 55106